Seasons

Thea Feldman

KINGFISHER

KINGFISHER

First published 2013 by Kingfisher
an imprint of Macmillan Children's Books
a division of Macmillan Publishers Limited
20 New Wharf Road, London N1 9RR
Basingstoke and Oxford
Associated companies throughout the world
www.panmacmillan.com

Series editor: Heather Morris
Literacy consultant: Hilary Horton

ISBN: 978-0-7534-3317-1
Copyright © Macmillan Children's Books 2013

9 8 7 6 5 4 3 2 1

1TR/1012/WKT/UG/105MA

A CIP catalogue record for this book is available from
the British Library.

Printed in China

Picture credits
The Publisher would like to thank the following for permission to reproduce their material.
Every care has been taken to trace copyright holders. However, if there have been unintentional
omissions or failure to trace copyright holders, we apologize and will, if informed, endeavour to make
corrections in any future edition.
Top = t; Bottom = b; Centre = c; Left = l; Right = r
Cover Shutterstock/cappi thompson; Pages 3 Getty/AFP; 4–5 Shutterstock/Kotenko Oleksandr;
6 Shutterstock/Liudmila Evdochimova; 7 Shutterstock/jordache; 8–9 Photolibrary/Imagebroker;
10–11 Photolibrary/Peter Arnold Images; 12 Photolibrary/Animals Animals; 13 Shutterstock/Mayovskyy
Andrew; 14 Shutterstock/Dmitry Naumov; 15 Photolibrary/DK Stock; 16 inset Shutterstock/Elena Elisseeva;
16 Shutterstock/WDG Photo; 17 Shutterstock/Irrinn0215; 18 Shutterstock/Margaret M Stewart;
19 Shutterstock/Vishnevskiy Vasily; 20–21 Alamy/Corbis Bridge; 22 Shutterstock/Sonya Etchison;
23 Photolibrary/Erik Isakson/Tetra; 24 Shutterstock/Lawrence Cruciana; 25 Shutterstock/nikkytok;
26–27 Alamy/Chad Ehlers; 28 Shutterstock/Subbotina Anna; 29t Corbis/Andrew Parkinson;
29b Shutterstock/Marty Ellis; 30c Photolibrary/Jose Luis Pelaez/Iconica; 30b Corbis/Ted Horowitz;
31c Shutterstock/Brocreative; 31b Corbis/ Dann Tardiff/ Blend

It is snowing!

What **season** is it?

It is **winter**!

It is cold in winter.

Snow can fall from the clouds.

Do you like snow?

When you go outside in winter you wear a warm coat.

You put on mittens and a hat.

You wear boots.

And you need a scarf too!

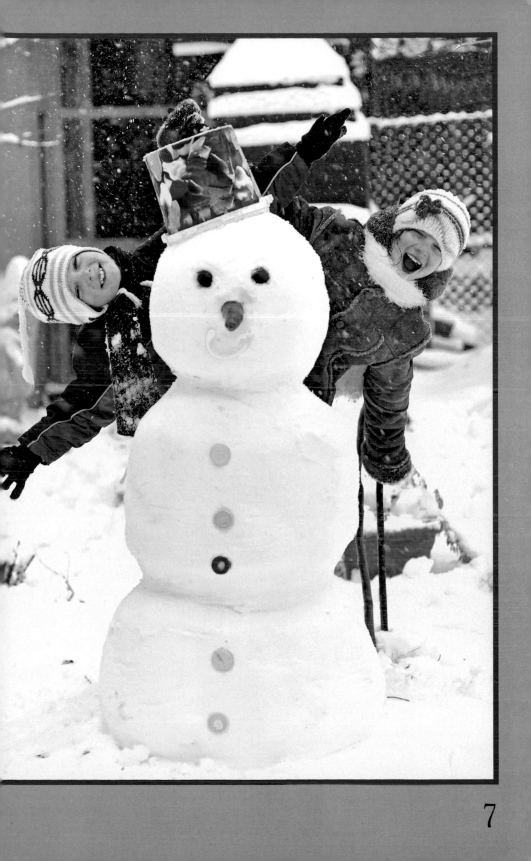

Outside, many trees are bare.

They have lost their leaves.

Many plants do not grow
flowers in winter.

The sun sets early in the
evening too.

Some animals find warm places
to sleep in winter.

These bears are sleeping
in a cave.

The animals will sleep
until winter is over.

Winter lasts three months.

What season comes
after winter?

Spring!

It gets warm in spring.

Sometimes it rains.

Sometimes the sun shines.

The days get longer.

In spring, new leaves
grow on trees.

New flowers grow on plants.

Animals wake up from their winter sleep.

Many animals have babies
in spring.

Spring lasts for three months.

What season comes after spring?

Summer!

It is hot in summer.

The sun is strong.

The days are long.

There is more time to play outside!

You have a break from school in summer.

What do you like to do instead?

You can have a picnic.

You can go swimming.

There are many fun things
to do!

Trees have green leaves
in summer.

Plants have colourful flowers.

Animals have a lot to eat.

Summer lasts for three months.

What season comes
after summer?

Autumn!

It is cool in autumn.

The wind blows more.

The days get shorter.

The sun sets earlier.

Leaves turn red,
yellow and brown.

Many plants stop
growing flowers.

Some birds fly away

Some animals gather food
for when autumn is over.

Autumn lasts for three months.

What season comes after
autumn?

Many places have four seasons.
Some places have fewer.

winter

spring

The seasons come one after another, year after year.

Which season do you like best?

summer

autumn

Glossary

autumn the season that comes after summer, when the weather gets cooler

season a time that can be several months long, when the same kind of weather happens every year

snow frozen water that falls from clouds as snowflakes

spring the season that comes after winter, when the weather starts to get warmer

summer the warmest season of the year

winter the coldest season of the year